Smithsonian

CURIOUS ABOUT MONEY

by Mary E. Reid

GROSSET & DUNLAP

An Imprint of Penguin Random House

GROSSET & DUNLAP

Penguin Young Readers Group
An Imprint of Penguin Random House LLC

● Smithsonian

This trademark is owned by the Smithsonian Institution and
is registered in the U.S. Patent and Trademark Office.

Smithsonian Enterprises:
Christopher Liedel, President
Carol LeBlanc, Senior Vice President, Education and Consumer Products
Brigid Ferraro, Vice President, Education and Consumer Products
Ellen Nanney, Licensing Manager
Kealy Gordon, Product Development Manager

- -

PHOTO CREDITS: LIBRARY OF CONGRESS: 7 (top), 15 (top), 16 (bottom), 18, 21 (top and bottom, left).
SMITHSONIAN NATIONAL MUSEUM OF AMERICAN HISTORY: front and back covers, 1 (top left and right, bottom
right), 3, 6, 7 (bottom), 8 (right), 9 (left), 10, 11, 12, 13, 14, 15 (bottom left), 16 (top left and right), 17 (top left and right),
19 (bottom, left, center, right), 20, 21 (top and bottom, right), 22, 23, 24 (bottom, all), 25 (top left and right), 26, 32.
THINKSTOCK: 1 (bottom left, photo by Maher), 8 (left, photo by Ingram Publishing), 9 (right, photo by Zack Frank), 17
(bottom, photo by Epitavi), 19 (top, photo by idal), 24 (top, photos by JordiDelgado; bottom left, photo by Devonyu), 25
(bottom, photo by Farzana Sadat), 27 (photos by Kary Nieuwenhuis), 28 (photo by Jitalia17), 29
(photo by Farzana Sadat), 30 (photo by Comstock), 31 (photo by arinahabich).

- -

Library of Congress Cataloging-in-Publication Data is available.

ISBN 978-1-101-99606-5   10 9 8 7 6 5 4 3 2 1

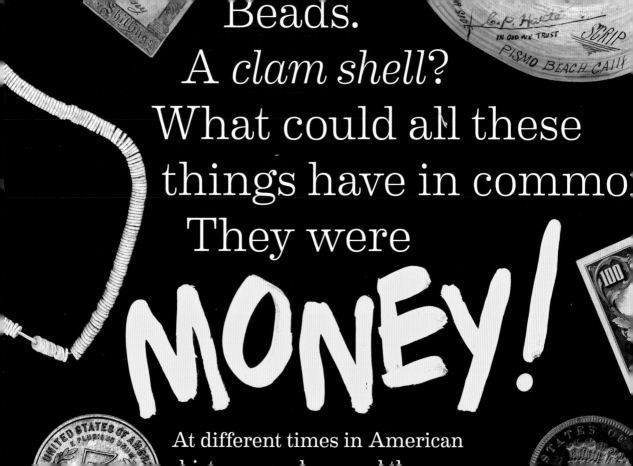

Beads.
A *clam shell*?
What could all these
things have in commo[n]
They were

MONEY!

At different times in American
hi[story people used these]

The people who settled in the thirteen colonies that became the United States had a money problem: not enough coins!

These colonies were once ruled by the king of England. Only he could order coins to be made. The American colonists had to use English coins—and there weren't enough of them to go around.

But the colonists knew there were other things people valued.

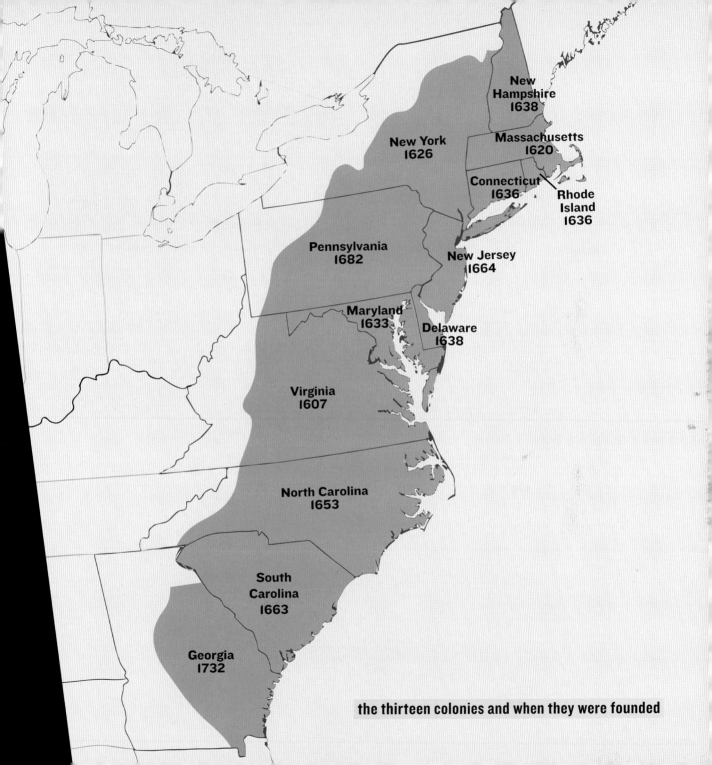

New
Hampshire
1638

New York
1626

Massachusetts
1620

Connecticut
1636

Rhode
Island
1636

Pennsylvania
1682

New Jersey
1664

Maryland
1633

Delaware
1638

Virginia
1607

North Carolina
1653

South
Carolina
1663

Georgia
1732

the thirteen colonies and when they were founded

a South American coin

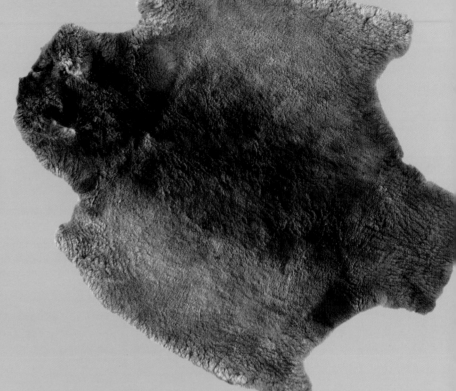

a beaver pelt (furry skin of the animal)

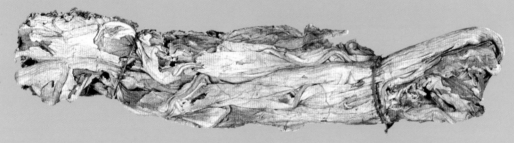

tobacco leaves

When they wanted to buy tea, cloth, paper, china, or more coins from England, the colonists sold shiploads of furs or tobacco to the English. They also used coins that came from trade in South America.

American Indians taught the colonists about using wampum. Wampum is beads made from shells. It was valuable and could be exchanged among people in different ways.

trading ships

wampum beads on a pelt

Imagine buying, selling, and trading things with all these different kinds of goods and money!

The colonists wanted to make their own coins, and some did. Clever colonists in Massachusetts created this pine-tree coin around 1670, but they put 1652 on it.

That's when there was no king in England because of a dispute. So the colonists could claim they had to make their own coins!

The pine tree stands for the trees sold for ships' masts, the tall poles that hold up the sails.

Even though some American colonists ignored the king's rule about creating coins, there still wasn't enough gold, silver, or copper to produce enough coins. But the king hadn't said anything about making *paper* money.

Philadelphia money showing the thirteen colonies

30-dollar bill, Philadelphia

People in the thirteen colonies got busy!

Some of the first paper money issued by a government in the Western world was printed in the Massachusetts colony. Other American colonies soon printed their own paper money, too.

30 shillings, New Jersey

15 shillings, Pennsylvania

Now there was a new problem: What was all this money worth?

Money looked different in different places. Paper money worth a certain amount in one colony might be worth something else in another colony. People made charts to help them compare values.

With so many different bills and coins, people could easily counterfeit or make fake money. Counterfeit money hurt the value of real money.

The colonists worked hard to prevent counterfeiting. They made bills with wavy edges at the top. If the wavy edge matched the edge in a government stub book, the money was real.

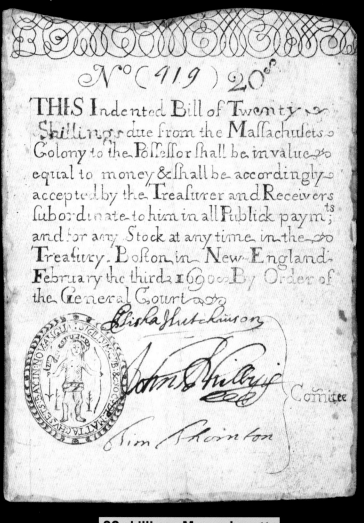

20 shillings, Massachusetts

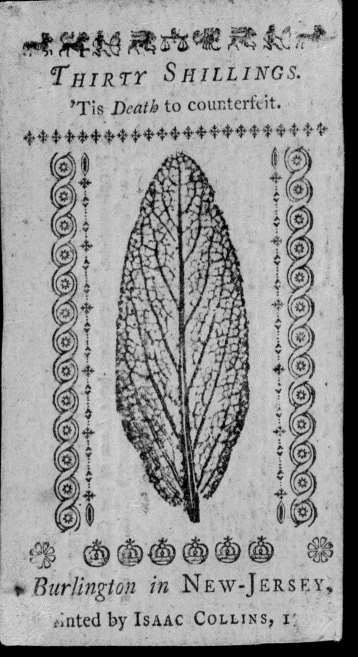

THIRTY SHILLINGS.

'Tis *Death* to counterfeit.

Burlington in NEW-JERSEY,

Printed by ISAAC COLLINS, 1

leaf-print money (1761)

Other bills were printed with small mistakes. The counterfeiters would miss them, and the fake money they printed wouldn't match real money.

Benjamin Franklin, the famous statesman and inventor, designed paper money with leaf prints on it. No two plant leaves are exactly alike, so these bills couldn't be copied. Other printers liked the idea.

From 1775 to 1783, the thirteen American colonies fought for
freedom from the English king. After they won the war, the former
colonists set up their own country, the United States of America. The
new government had to decide many things, including what money
to use.

Signing the Declaration of Independence

In 1792, Congress (the lawmaking branch of the government) created the United States Mint. This "money factory" would produce gold, silver, and copper coins. Now everybody in the new nation would be able to use the same coins.

President George Washington inspects the first US coins

the first Mint building

The Mint was built in Philadelphia, which was then the capital of the United States.

one of the first **US** pennies (1793)

first **US** half dime (1794)

Thomas Jefferson (1743–1826)

Thomas Jefferson, a Founding Father and government leader, helped figure out what the new United States money would be worth.

The basic unit would be a 1-dollar coin. Other coins would be worth a part, or fraction, of 1 dollar. The 25-cent coin was a "quarter" of a dollar. The "half dime" was the first 5-cent coin. There was also a penny and a halfpenny.

US quarter dollar (1796)

first US silver dollar (1794)

Congress voted this money system into law in 1792. But the new United States still didn't have a lot of metal for coins. President George Washington and his wife, Martha Washington, may have given the Mint their silverware to be melted down for coins!

Gold!

In 1848, this valuable metal was discovered in California and later, Alaska. Silver was mined in the Rocky Mountains. Metal meant money—and not just for the miners!

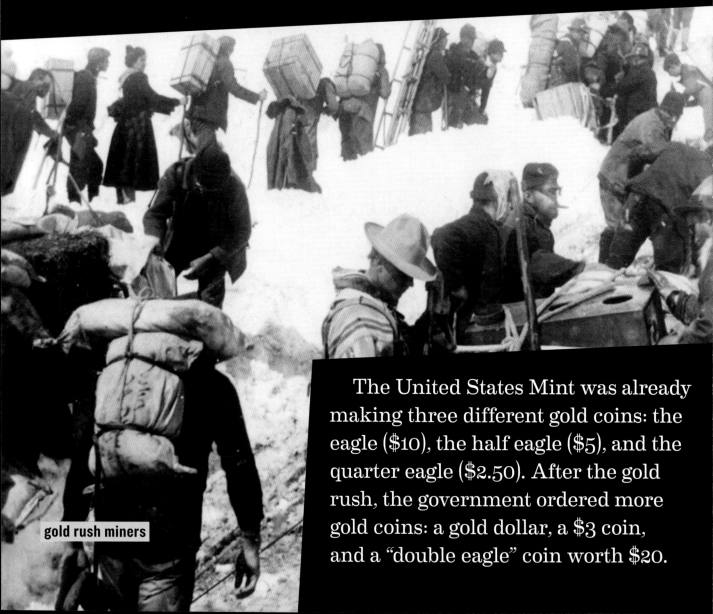

gold rush miners

The United States Mint was already making three different gold coins: the eagle ($10), the half eagle ($5), and the quarter eagle ($2.50). After the gold rush, the government ordered more gold coins: a gold dollar, a $3 coin, and a "double eagle" coin worth $20.

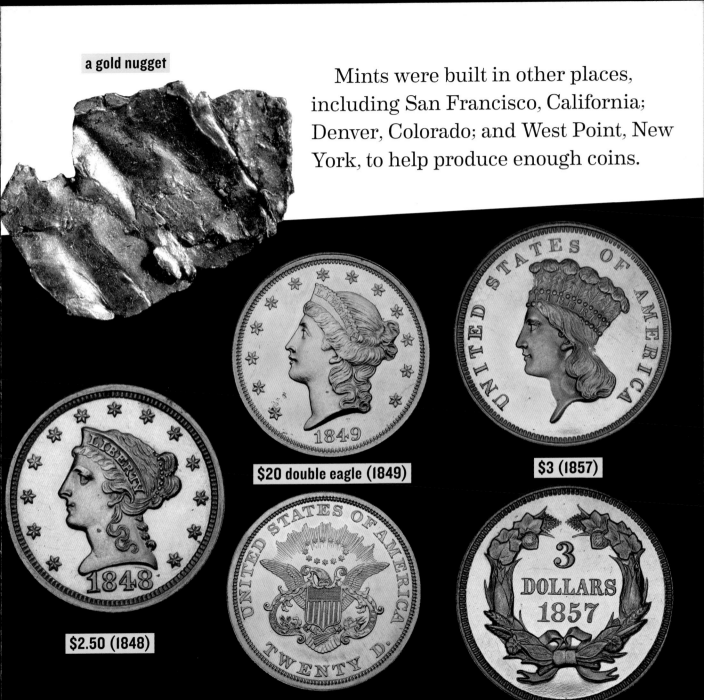

a gold nugget

Mints were built in other places, including San Francisco, California; Denver, Colorado; and West Point, New York, to help produce enough coins.

$20 double eagle (1849)

$3 (1857)

$2.50 (1848)

The new system of national coins worked well. But the states continued to print their own paper money. There were still many different bills. About one-third of them were counterfeit! Something had to be done.

In the 1860s, Congress decided that only the central government should issue paper money. Bills as large as $10,000 and $100,000 were printed. Now the United States was really united by a complete money system.

The $100,000 bill was only printed in 1934.

Coins were still produced. One beautiful gold coin was designed by an artist. President Theodore Roosevelt asked a famous sculptor, Augustus Saint-Gaudens, to plan a new coin. It became the famous double eagle of 1907.

Augustus Saint-Gaudens (1848–1907)

Theodore Roosevelt (1858–1919)

Saint-Gaudens's $20 double eagle. There were many more copies made of a flatter version of this coin.

1794

1804

1838

Another part of the 1792 law that created the money system in the United States said all national coins should include the word liberty and a picture of "Lady Liberty." This showed what the founders thought was most important about the new country. The word *liberty* is still on American coins today.

1854

1921

1907

Lady Liberty was joined by the American bald eagle. Congress had chosen the eagle as the national bird because it was fierce and powerful. But that's not exactly what the first eagles on coins looked like!

Over time, pictures of other ideas, people, or events that were important in American history were printed on paper money or stamped on coins.

Susan B. Anthony fought to get American women the right to vote.
She was the first real woman to appear on an American coin.
The back honors the US moon landing in 1969.

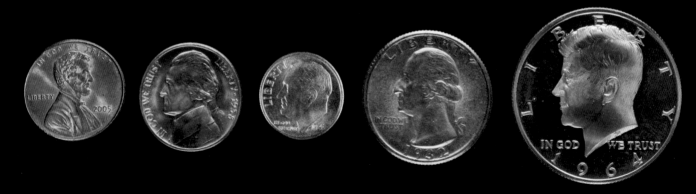

Several US coins show a president: Abraham Lincoln (penny),
Thomas Jefferson (nickel), Franklin Roosevelt (dime), George
Washington (quarter), and John F. Kennedy (half dollar).

Lakota Sioux chief Iron Tail and Cheyenne chief Two Moons were models for this "buffalo" nickel.

Remember Benjamin Franklin and his leaf-print bill you couldn't counterfeit? Now he's on a $100 bill. It is also designed to be hard to counterfeit.

Money talks . . . about history! That's why some people collect it.

Thomas Jefferson gathered coins from around the world. This helped him in planning the money for the new United States.

People also collect rare coins because they are valuable. A rare coin can be one with a mistake on it, or one of which only a few were made. The 1849 double-eagle-pattern coin is the only one in the world. That's rare! It was made as a tryout for a new coin that was made the next year.

the rare double-eagle pattern (1849)

state quarters

America the Beautiful quarters

Some people collect money to show where they have been. Other people collect coins because they are interesting. For example, some quarters honor the fifty states or show many of the amazing places in the United States.

Money doesn't just change hands—it's always changing. And sometimes it becomes more valuable than itself!

By 1965, the silver in dimes and quarters was worth more than the coins. President Lyndon B. Johnson ordered that the dime and the quarter be made of cheaper material. These "sandwich" coins are copper in the middle and silver-colored metal on the outside.

It's harder to make fake money now, too. New $5, $10, $20, $50, and $100 bills are printed with secret ink colors. They are made of a special material that has red and blue threads in it. It is so strong that a bill can be folded about four thousand times before it tears.

These new bills also have a 3-D strip in them. All of these things show the money is real and make it hard to counterfeit.

Technology is changing how people use money, too. People don't even need to use coins or bills if they don't want to. They can write a paper check or swipe a plastic credit or debit card to pay for something. Or they can use computers to move money in and out of their bank, pay bills, or buy and sell things online.

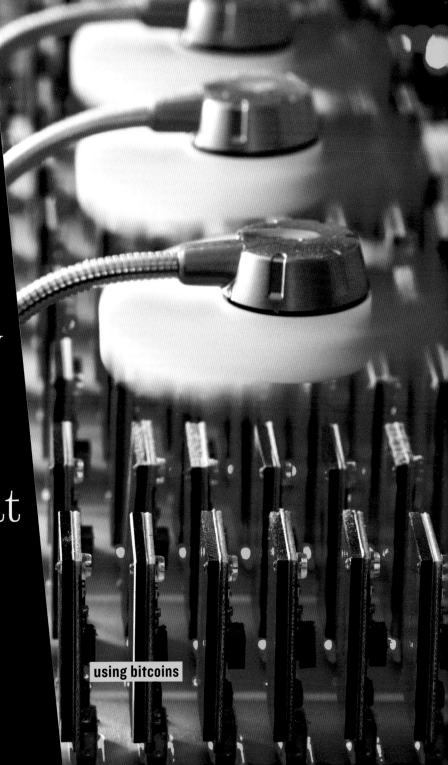

Bitcoin is one of several kinds of electronic money. They're not real coins—but you can use bitcoins to pay for things on the Internet. And you keep your bitcoins in an electronic wallet!

We still talk about the value of American money in "dollars and cents."

But who knows what money will look like in the future!

using bitcoins

GLOSSARY

colonies: places that are ruled by another country

colonists: people who live in colonies

copper: a reddish-colored metal

counterfeit: fake; meant to look like something in order to trick people

debit card: a plastic payment card linked to a source of money

Founding Father: one of the men who helped set up the United States of America

fraction: part of something

issued: put something out or produced something

liberty: freedom to speak and act as you want to

national: belonging to or about a whole nation or country

produce: to make something

technology: tools or a way of doing something, which today is often electronic

value: what something is worth

wampum: beads made from shells that had value